Original title:

Fallow Mandrakes Under the Dragon Bulb

Author: Sara Säde

ISBN HARDBACK: 978-1-80562-078-5

ISBN PAPERBACK: 978-1-80563-599-4

The Eulogy of the Slumbering Bulb

In twilight's grasp, the bulb does rest,
A slumber deep, in nature's breast.
Fingers of earth cradle its dreams,
While starlit whispers weave in streams.

Time ticks softly, a clock of moss,
Guardian shadows, forgive the gloss.
Gentle rains sweep the dust away,
For life awaits the break of day.

Secrets pulse in the soil's hold,
Stories of warmth, still yet untold.
Awake shall bloom the colors bright,
As dawn unfolds its vibrant light.

In silence deep, the roots entwine,
Casting a bond through dark, divine.
Sprouts of hope stretch towards the sun,
While life and death become as one.

Dreamscape of the Rooted Abyss

In realms below, the shadows dance,
Roots entwine in a timeless trance.
Whispers echo through earth's embrace,
A tapestry woven in secret space.

Beneath the world, where silence breathes,
Dreams are sown like autumn leaves.
Crimson wishes, in darkness splayed,
Befriend the night where fate has laid.

The heart of earth, a pulsing thread,
Awakened visions where spirits tread.
In murky depths, the lost finds grace,
As stars descend to kiss their face.

Traces linger on paths unseen,
Shapes of wonders lost in between.
An ode to shadows, they serenade,
In the rooted abyss, dawn shall cascade.

The Melody of the Withering Grove

In the grove where the aged stand,
Leaves will flutter like the sighing hand.
Echoes of laughter from times gone by,
Murmuring secrets to the sky.

Birch and oak with wisdom old,
Tales of love and loss retold.
The rustling breeze a mournful tune,
As twilight wraps the world in gloom.

Every branch bends beneath the weight,
Of memories lingered in silent fate.
Light dances softly through golden hues,
Where shadows whisper their tender dues.

In the twilight's reach, colors bleed,
Withering forms from life's last seed.
Yet in decay, there's beauty spun,
In the cycle of life, all must run.

Rhapsody of the Silent Vines

In tangled tendrils, dreams entwine,
A serenade of the silent vine.
Gentle breezes caress the green,
Whispers fleeting, barely seen.

Climbing high in a lover's grace,
Seeking warmth in a sunlit placc.
With each twist, a secret keeps,
In the garden where stillness sleeps.

Time meanders in leafy curls,
While nature spins its silent pearls.
Under the moon's watchful gaze,
The vines weave tales of ancient days.

Beneath the stars, they stretch and sway,
Unfolding night into the day.
A rhapsody sung through the leaves,
Of whispered hope the heart believes.

Convergence of the Hidden Pathways

In shadows deep where whispers dwell,
The ancient ways begin to swell.
With secrets held by moonlit skies,
The hidden truths before our eyes.

Through twisted vines and paths long lost,
Each footstep taken bears a cost.
Yet in the dark, a glimmer glows,
A flicker where the starlight flows.

With every breath, the night unfolds,
As stories speak of brave and bold.
In unity, these trails align,
A convergence lost to eyes, divine.

The rustling leaves in sighs convey,
The tales of yesteryear's array.
With every corner turned anew,
Adventures wait, a world askew.

So take the hand of fate's embrace,
And trust the heart to guide through space.
For on this route of whispered fate,
The paths entwine, they do not wait.

Echoes of the Celestial Harvest

Beneath the stars, a bounty glows,
In fields where twilight river flows.
Each grain of light, a story spun,
A radiant dance 'twixt moon and sun.

The harvest beckons, echoes clear,
Of whispered hopes and silent fear.
In shadowed corners, dreams take flight,
As constellations weave through night.

With every touch of golden grain,
The songs of old whisper in vain.
In twilight's glow, hearts come alive,
As spirits stir where visions thrive.

The universe, a tapestry bright,
Intertwines the dark and light.
Through every thread, the cosmos weaves,
The echoes borne by autumn leaves.

So gather 'round and heed the call,
In every voice, we hear it all.
The celestial harvest, rich and vast,
In unity, we hold it fast.

Ephemeral Roots of Forgotten Realms

In ancient woods where memories flow,
The roots of tales begin to grow.
Each whisper shrouded, held in time,
The echoes speak, a soft chime.

Beneath the surface, shadows creep,
In realms of magic, secrets sleep.
With fragile threads of golden dew,
The past entwines, a dream in hue.

In twilight's breath, the stories bloom,
Of distant lands that spell impending doom.
Yet in their depths, hope flickers bright,
To guide the lost through endless night.

With every turn in twisted bark,
The world unfolds, igniting spark.
For in forgotten realms, we find,
The fleeting roots that bind mankind.

So wander close and keep in mind,
The ephemeral paths that twist and wind.
For every journey bears a thread,
To tie us to the paths once tread.

The Veiled Dance of the Blooms

In gardens lush where shadows play,
The blooms unfold at close of day.
With petals soft like whispers sigh,
They dance beneath the twilight sky.

Each blossom speaks in colors bright,
A secret song of day and night.
With gentle motion, they take flight,
In harmony, a pure delight.

The moonlight weaves through leaves that twine,
As starlit paths begin to shine.
In every twirl, the blooms embrace,
The magic held in nature's grace.

Yet hidden deep, the shadows loom,
A veiled dance conceals the gloom.
In every petal's soft caress,
Lies the power to transgress.

So linger here, dear friend of mine,
In blooms that dance and intertwine.
For in their sway, a truth is found,
The veiled secrets of the ground.

The Tangle of the Dreaming Roots

In the glade where whispers play,
Dreaming roots weave night and day.
Beneath the soil, secrets hide,
In shadows deep, the echoes bide.

Winds carry tales from the trees,
Swirling softly, like autumn leaves.
The tangled thoughts of ages past,
In every knot, a spell is cast.

Moonlit paths of silken thread,
Guide the wanderer, the dreamer led.
Through the labyrinth of the night,
To find the dawn, a beacon bright.

Footfalls soft as a lullaby,
In the murmur, hear the sigh.
Roots of dreams entwined in fate,
Awake the magic, before it's late.

In the tapestry of time,
Stories whisper, rhythm and rhyme.
From tangled roots our dreams ascend,
Forever bound, yet never end.

The Silent Call of the Earth's Heart

Beneath the surface, pulses beat,
A silent call, both soft and sweet.
The earth's heart whispers in the dark,
To those who seek the quiet spark.

With every step upon the ground,
A symphony of life is found.
The quiet hum of roots below,
In stillness, ancient secrets flow.

Gentle breezes carry the tune,
In twilight's glow, beneath the moon.
The call of earth, both fierce and mild,
In every heart, a wonder wild.

Listen closely, hear the song,
The earth's heartbeat, steady and strong.
Through every shadow, every light,
It guides us gently through the night.

As the stars twinkle in their dance,
We follow fate's enchanted chance.
In silence, answers will impart,
The beautiful call of the earth's heart.

The Cradle of Myths and Roots

In the cradle where legends lie,
Myths entwined as seasons fly.
From whispering leaves, stories rise,
Beneath the vast, eternal skies.

Old tales told by firelight,
In shadows cast, a glimpse of sight.
The roots that anchor, deep and wide,
Hold every truth that time can bide.

Each branch a tale, each leaf a verse,
In nature's song, we find the curse.
To wander through the age-old woods,
Is to embrace what once was good.

In the cradle's arms, we dream and sigh,
While ancient voices softly cry.
Roots of history veil our past,
In every heartbeat, shadows cast.

So gather close, let myths unfold,
In every whisper, legends told.
With hands entwined, we find our way,
In the cradle of roots, myths hold sway.

Shadows of the Luminescent Bulb

In twilight's glow, a bulb doth shine,
Casting shadows, long and fine.
In stillness, secrets softly creep,
Awakening dreams from restless sleep.

With every flicker, a story starts,
Illuminating the hidden parts.
The shadows dance, a waltz of light,
In the quiet depths of the night.

Beneath each beam, a world lies bare,
Of whispered hopes and silent care.
The bulb's soft glow, a guardian bright,
Guides us gently through the night.

In corners dark, where phantoms play,
The luminescent glimmers sway.
With every pulse, a heartbeat's breath,
In light we find the charms of death.

So in this glow, let shadows speak,
Of truths and tales, both brave and meek.
In the dance of light, we find our fate,
In shadows cast, we contemplate.

Whispers of the Hidden Roots

Beneath the ground where secrets lie,
The ancient roots weave tales so spry.
In murmurs soft, the echoes swirl,
Revealing worlds in twilight's whirl.

In shadows deep, the whispers flow,
Of hidden paths where few dare go.
Each tendril speaks of time long past,
A history woven, vast and vast.

The moon above, its glow so bright,
Illuminates the hidden sight.
While creatures dance on silent wings,
Their magic sings of wondrous things.

With every breath, the night unveils,
A tapestry of whispered tales.
The roots entwined in earth's embrace,
Reveal the wonders of this place.

So wander here, where shadows play,
And let the ancient roots convey.
In secret whispers, find your way,
For magic stirs at end of day.

Shadows Beneath the Ancient Grove

In the grove where shadows sigh,
The air is thick with secrets nigh.
Beneath the boughs, a tale unfolds,
Of whispered dreams and legends bold.

The branches sway, a gentle muse,
While twilight paints in dusky hues.
A flicker here, a shimmer there,
Invisible threads weave through the air.

The heart of night remembers well,
The stories of the earth to tell.
Each rustle speaks of days long gone,
As evening breathes its quiet yawn.

With every step on mossy ground,
The echoes of the past surround.
In shadows draped, enchantments dwell,
In ancient oak, a mystic spell.

So linger here, where time is lost,
Embrace the beauty, heed the cost.
For those who seek with open eyes,
Shall find the truth that never dies.

Secrets of the Nightshade Garden

In the garden where nightshades grow,
A tapestry of secrets, aglow.
With petals dark and leaves of green,
The hidden magic can be seen.

Among the blooms, a silence hums,
As whispered chants from shadow comes.
The moonlight dances on the stems,
Awaking ancient, mystic gems.

Each leaf a letter, each root a line,
Tales of the lost intertwine.
Within this vale, where dreams reside,
The truth of nature cannot hide.

So bend your ear and listen well,
To secrets that the night will tell.
In fragrance soft, the spirits play,
Unraveling night from the day.

And as you wander, take your time,
For magic lives in every rhyme.
The nightshade whispers sweet and low,
In the garden, truth shall grow.

Echoes of the Forgotten Harvest

Where fields once thrived in golden grain,
Echoes linger, sweet with pain.
Forgotten harvests, tales untold,
Of warmth and labor, brave and bold.

The twilight casts a gentle hue,
As whispers weave through vale and dew.
In the distance, the haunting song,
Of seasons passing, right and wrong.

Each grain a story, each stalk a dream,
Of laughter shared and sunlit gleam.
Yet shadows mask what once was bright,
In echoes soft of fading light.

The earth remembers, though we forget,
The hands that toiled in sun and fret.
In every rustle, a prayer remains,
For echoes linger, despite the chains.

So honor those who came before,
With hearts of courage, rich in lore.
For in the harvest, life abounds,
In echoes deep, the world resounds.

Echoing Lullabies of the Cursed Grove

In shadows deep where whispers creep,
The nightingale weeps, the secrets keep.
Moonlight dances on the willow's weave,
A lullaby sung, for those who grieve.

The trees stand tall, with bark like scars,
Echoing dreams of forgotten stars.
Each rustling leaf a tale untold,
In winds of sorrow, the heart takes hold.

A mist embraces the cobblestone path,
As shadows gather, igniting wrath.
Ghostly figures sway with the breeze,
In the cursed grove, no soul finds ease.

The echoes call to the brave and bold,
Their stories flow, like rivers of gold.
In every corner, a haunting song,
Of echoes lost, where shadows belong.

With every note, the darkness stirs,
A symphony sung as the night concurs.
Close your eyes; let the lullabies flow,
In the grove, where the cursed winds blow.

The Dreamweaver's Botanical Secrets

In the garden where dreams are sown,
The Dreamweaver spins tales unknown.
Petals flutter like whispers of fate,
Awakening visions, oh, so sedate.

Each flower blooms with a secret bight,
Colors twinkle in soft twilight.
With a touch of magic, the leaves conspire,
To unveil the dreams that hearts desire.

Beneath the moon's gentle embrace,
The garden reveals its hidden grace.
Honeyed fragrances fill the air,
As starlit dreams become a snare.

Roots entwined in a dance of fate,
Every bloom a portal to navigate.
Wander lightly, let your spirit roam,
In the world of dreams, find your home.

The garden whispers with a knowing glance,
As shadows thrum in a timeless dance.
Unlock the secrets, let them ignite,
For in this realm, the soul takes flight.

Ascent of the Eternal Roots

In ancient woods, where silence broods,
The roots ascend, igniting moods.
Beneath the earth, they twist and turn,
In the dark soil, the flames do burn.

Every knot tells of journeys past,
Whispered secrets in shadows cast.
Searching deep for the light above,
Eternal hope, as roots entwine love.

From the forest floor to the sky's expanse,
Roots embrace a forgotten dance.
With resolute strength, they reach for the stars,
Each path they forge heals old scars.

Nature's pulse in the silent ground,
The hidden songs of life resound.
Reach up high, let your spirit soar,
In the ascent of roots, find your core.

The cycles turn in harmony's song,
Where all belong, where heartbeats throng.
Follow the roots, let the journey start,
For in their embrace, all paths impart.

The Language of Silent Buds

In the stillness, the buds emerge,
A silent language begins to surge.
Petals whisper secrets soft and low,
In the quiet dance, new life will grow.

Each tender shoot holds the world inside,
An unspoken story, a blooming tide.
With patience, they wait for the sun's embrace,
To share their beauty, to find their place.

Through gentle rains and the warmest breeze,
The buds awaken, their hearts at ease.
In every color, a tale unfolds,
The language of flowers, as time beholds.

Roots beneath murmur in silent cheer,
As buds unfurl, what was once unclear.
Nature's expression, a soft, sweet hymn,
In the garden of dreams, where hopes swim.

Listen close; let the silence speak,
In the language of buds, find the unique.
For every blossom brings light anew,
In the dance of silence, love finds you.

Echoes of the Twilight Fertility

In the hush of twilight's song,
Soft whispers drift where shadows throng.
Beneath the moon's embrace, they swell,
Secrets echo where dreams compel.

The earth, a quilt of hidden grace,
Cradles life in its warm embrace.
Fertile grounds where magpies soar,
Call for blossoms to wake once more.

As starlight weaves a silver thread,
Crimson blooms in twilight spread.
With every tug of nature's hand,
Hope rises gently from the land.

In a valiant dance, they intertwine,
Roots and tendrils, sun and brine.
Lost in this verdant symphony,
Nature's pulse is wild and free.

So listen close as whispers fall,
The twilight waits, a beckoning call.
With every heartbeat, love transcends,
In echoes sweet, the twilight bends.

A Reverie for the Blossomless

In a garden bare, where silence sighs,
The weight of emptiness quietly lies.
Amidst the stones where shadows creep,
Memories linger, yet dreams sleep.

The barren branches stretch and plead,
For the gentle kiss of sun and seed.
In whispered tones of yesteryear,
A tender hope both bright and clear.

As the winds carry a mournful tune,
Lamenting the loss beneath the moon.
Yet in this void, a spark remains,
A flicker of life hidden in chains.

For flowers wait beneath the frost,
In silent vigil for what is lost.
With every heartbeat, they yearn to sprout,
A fragrant promise, cast about.

In time's embrace, their truth will bloom,
To banish sorrow, dispel the gloom.
And in that grace, the blossomless,
Shall join the dance, their fate a caress.

Secrets of the Forgotten Gourds

In the maze of vines, where shadows twine,
Ancient secrets in whispers align.
Beneath the leaves that softly sway,
Forgotten gourds have lost their way.

Once vibrant orbs, like souls concealed,
In twilight's haze, their fate revealed.
Time has etched its tale in lines,
Of gourd-shaped dreams that fate entwines.

They hold the laughter of autumn's kiss,
In every curve, a stolen bliss.
Yet in their silence, a story keeps,
Of harvest moons and midnight sweeps.

When lantern light dances on the ground,
The echoes of joy can still be found.
In faded hues, they speak the past,
Of love and loss, of time that's vast.

So let us listen to their lore,
In shadows cast from days of yore.
For in the silence, they softly sing,
Of forgotten hope each autumn brings.

Ensnared in the Whispering Vines

Beneath the boughs where shadows cling,
A tale unfolds, a haunting ring.
In the depths of twilight's embrace,
Whispering vines weave dreams of grace.

Tangled roots and stories breathe,
Lost in the dance of tangled wreath.
A symphony sung in moonlit night,
Secrets rustle in gentle flight.

With every twist, a mystery grows,
In emerald cloaks, the silence throes.
Tales of fate, both fierce and kind,
Entwined together, hearts aligned.

As shadows wane, the dawn draws near,
The whispers fade, yet still we hear.
For in the dance of nature's hand,
Love holds sway, eternally planned.

So let the vines ensnare your soul,
In whispered dreams, find yourself whole.
In every curl, a hope confined,
A glorious truth, forever entwined.

Murmurs in the Twilight Vale

In the vale where shadows play,
Whispers drift at end of day.
Crickets sing a lullaby,
As stars awaken in the sky.

Moonlight dances on the stream,
Casting spells in silver gleam.
Trees sway gently, soft and low,
Holding secrets none may know.

A breeze carries tales of old,
Of magic lost and dreams untold.
A flicker here, a shimmer there,
In twilight's grasp, all hearts laid bare.

The night unfolds its velvet curtain,
Where hopes and wishes lie for certain.
Each sigh and murmur, soft and light,
In this deep vale, shadows take flight.

So linger awhile, dear heart,
Embrace the wonders, let them start.
For in this vale, life's tender sway,
Holds magic hidden, night and day.

The Enchanted Expanse of Dusk

As dusk descends, the world transforms,
Colors blaze in vibrant swarms.
The horizon whispers tales anew,
In the enchanted evening hue.

Fireflies dance in playful flight,
Guided by the soft twilight.
Every flicker, a wish made true,
In this expanse, dreams come to view.

The land is cloaked in mystery,
Bound by the threads of history.
Crimson skies and velvet seas,
Speak of magic on the breeze.

Each moment holds a spark divine,
A glimpse of fate's design.
In shadows deep, the heart will soar,
As dusk unfolds its secret door.

So wander forth, let spirits guide,
Through the expanse where wonders bide.
In whispers soft, and twilight's glow,
The enchanted paths of dusk will show.

Echoes of Long Forgotten Growth

In the forest, silence sings,
Of ancient roots and timeless things.
Echoes stir in leafy crowns,
Carried forth by gentle loons.

Little seeds that dared to dream,
Now sway in sunlight's golden beam.
Whispers hidden in the earth,
Recall the tales of life and birth.

A mossy carpet, soft and deep,
With every breath, the woods do keep.
Each rustle, a story to unfold,
Of vibrant lives both young and old.

In shadows cast by towering trees,
Lie the echoes of the breeze.
Future blooms in soil take flight,
Find their way in soft twilight.

So pause and listen, hearts alive,
In the growth where memories thrive.
For in the woods, where stories blend,
Lie the echoes that never end.

The Hidden Cradle of Life

Nestled deep where silence grows,
Lies a cradle no one knows.
In the heart of nature's sigh,
Life awakens, shy and spry.

Gentle streams like silver threads,
Weave through mossy, emerald beds.
Every droplet, a lullaby,
Sung in harmony with the sky.

In the shadows, life blooms bright,
Holding secrets wrapped in light.
From tiniest seed to grandest tree,
All find solace, wild and free.

The whispering winds, a soft embrace,
Cradle all within their grace.
In hidden corners, magic thrives,
Guarding the joy of tender lives.

So seek the cradle, small and rare,
Where life's wonders dwell with care.
For in each leaf and sway of vine,
Lies a world both yours and mine.

Secrets of the Dragon's Whisper

In shadows deep where secrets lie,
The dragon's breath begins to sigh.
With scales that shimmer, eyes alight,
It guards the truth that takes to flight.

Through tangled roots and ancient trees,
The whispers ride upon the breeze.
A riddle wrapped in scales so old,
Of treasures lost and tales retold.

Each heartbeat drips with magic rare,
A dance of fire in the air.
The curious dare to seek the flame,
But few return to speak its name.

So heed the tales of skies at dawn,
For dragons rise, and kingdoms spawn.
In every flame, a story glows,
Of mighty beasts and hidden foes.

Embrace the night, the secrets shared,
In whispered words, the brave have dared.
The dragon's whisper calls to thee,
Unlock the door to mystery.

The Truth Beneath the Tangled Green

In emerald depths where shadows blend,
A tapestry of truths descend.
The roots entwined, the stories weave,
In every leaf, secrets believe.

Through sunlight's dance and whispered breeze,
The forest breathes with ancient ease.
Each path a portal, wild and free,
To worlds unseen, to destiny.

Beneath the surface, magic stirs,
The truth unfolds in gentle purrs.
With every footfall softly made,
The heart of nature's game is played.

So tread with care, and hear the sound,
Of life unfolding all around.
For in the green, the wisdom flows,
A quest for truth that nature knows.

Embrace the quiet, listen close,
To murmurs sweet, the forest's prose.
In tangled green, where spirits roam,
You may just find that you are home.

Beneath the Kaleidoscope of Dreams

In twilight's glow where visions blend,
A kaleidoscope begins to send.
Through swirling hues and whispered sighs,
The canvas stretches past the skies.

With every thought, a color spins,
A tapestry where life begins.
The dreams take flight, and shadows play,
In vibrant dance, both night and day.

In secret corners of the mind,
The universe waits, unconfined.
With every heartbeat, stories bloom,
In colors bright that chase the gloom.

So close your eyes and let it flow,
Embrace the wonders yet to know.
In dreams, we find the truest gold,
A realm of magic, brave and bold.

Beneath the stars, we weave our fate,
In dreams, our hearts and hopes await.
So take a step, and dare to soar,
For dreams unlock an endless door.

The Harrowing Gaze of Earth's Watcher

From mountaintop with gaze so keen,
The Earth looks down, a watchful queen.
With ancient eyes that see it all,
It knows the rise, the destined fall.

Through whispered winds and sighing trees,
The watcher knows the world's decrees.
With every storm, with every sun,
A tale of life already spun.

In shadows cast and light that fades,
The watcher weeps for dreams that jade.
The cycles weave in dusk and dawn,
For in its gaze, all souls are drawn.

So heed the lessons etched in stone,
The watcher guides, but walks alone.
With every heartbeat, truth reveals,
The bonds we share, the love that heals.

Through seasons' change and time's embrace,
The Earth holds fast with stoic grace.
In its gaze lies a story vast,
A promise made that will hold fast.

Whispers of the Hidden Grove

In the grove where shadows play,
The soft winds sing a dulcet lay.
Whispers dance on leaves so fine,
Secret tales of the ancient pine.

Mossy stones and winding paths,
Heartbeats echo nature's laughs.
Flickering lights sway to and fro,
Inviting souls to gently flow.

Creatures peek from burrows deep,
Guarding dreams that softly seep.
Moonlit glimmers, softly spun,
Kissing night till day's begun.

Every rustle tells a story,
Of forgotten lines and hidden glory.
In this place where magic thrives,
Nature breathes, and wonder lives.

So wander forth, but heed the call,
For the grove will hold you in its thrall.
Lose yourself in the gentle night,
And find your heart in mystic light.

Secrets of the Twilight Flora

In twilight's grasp, where shadows blend,
The secrets of the sylvan tend.
Petals whisper, colors gleam,
Carrying tales of a hidden dream.

Dewdrops shimmer on silken strands,
Nature's ledger in delicate hands.
Every bloom a tale to weave,
Of love and loss, of those who grieve.

Beneath the boughs of ancient trees,
The air is sweet with magic's tease.
Fragrant notes of time long past,
In twilight's breath, forever cast.

Flickering lights of evening fair,
Invite the wonder and the dare.
Each step forward, a path unknown,
In twilight's song, our hearts are sown.

So glean the whispers from the night,
Where every shadow hints at light.
In flora's heart, deep secrets bloom,
As twilight flowers chase the gloom.

Shadows in the Dragon's Lair

In caverns deep where shadows creep,
Draconic dreams in silence sleep.
Rumbles echo, treasure glows,
Guarded fiercely, no one knows.

Scales of gold and piercing gaze,
Ancient tales of wildest days.
In the hollow, shadows sway,
Marking paths that none may stay.

Flickers of flame in the inky tide,
Breathtaking power the night can't hide.
With every heartbeat, secrets swell,
In dragon's roar, enchantments dwell.

Legends bound in dust and stone,
Echoes of battles fought and won.
In labyrinths, daring hearts must dance,
Chasing the shadows for the chance.

So tread with care in the dim-lit hall,
Where dragons whisper their ancient call.
Beneath the weight of time laid bare,
Are the shadows in the dragon's lair.

Enchantment of the Sleepy Roots

Beneath the trees where stillness reigns,
The sleepy roots weave their faint trains.
Tiny wonders in the earth,
Hold the murmurs of gentle birth.

Whispers wrap 'round weary feet,
Songs of solace, soft and sweet.
Cradled low where dreams entwine,
In each turn, a twist divine.

Mossy blankets gently sigh,
As if to cradle dreams that fly.
Every heartbeat echoes low,
In enchanted roots, where wonder grows.

Twilight dances on tender leaves,
Casting spells as night retrieves.
Resting hearts find peace anew,
In the sheltering of twilit hue.

So linger long in nature's care,
Let the magic spark and flare.
For in this world of whispered lore,
The sleepy roots will ask for more.

The Enigma of the Buried Bloom

In shadowed glades where whispers weave,
The secrets of the earth believe.
A flower sleeps beneath the stone,
In silence, guards its truth alone.

With roots that twist like ancient fates,
It dreams of time and opened gates.
A gentle breeze stirs memories,
As moonlight dances through the trees.

Each petal holds a tale untold,
Of love and loss, both warm and cold.
It waits for hands that seek to find,
The buried heart, the lost and blind.

Through thorns and brambles it shall grow,
A testament to all we sow.
And when at last the dawn breaks clear,
The bloom shall rise, dispelling fear.

From soil deep, the magic flows,
A haunting hymn the garden knows.
In twilight's glow, the truth shall bloom,
An enigma lost to time's dark loom.

Beneath the Veil of Moonlit Soil

Beneath the soft and silver light,
The earth conceals its sacred plight.
In layers thick, each secret lies,
Awaiting sun, awaiting skies.

The tendrils grasp, the shadows creep,
Through silent paths where whispers sleep.
A symphony of quiet dreams,
In darkness found, in moonlight beams.

Each whisper tells of ancient woes,
Of roots entwined and lost repose.
In solace sought, the earth will yield,
The magic trapped within the field.

Among the burrows, kinship grows,
With every twist, the mystery flows.
In gentle puffs of evening air,
The songs of nature fill the lair.

And as the night unfolds its shroud,
The soil breathes, both soft and loud.
A dance of shadows, life restored,
Beneath the veil, forever poured.

Serpents in the Twilight Orchard

In twilight's grasp, the orchard sighs,
With fruit so ripe beneath dark skies.
Where serpents slither, shadows glide,
In whispered tales, the secrets hide.

Each rustling leaf, a voice, a plea,
Entranced by fate, by destiny.
The apples gleam with mystery,
A taste of truth, a history.

Beneath the arches, magic brews,
With serpents weaving through the hues.
They guard the lore of days gone by,
And watch the stars prepare to fly.

In moonlit steps, the night will spark,
As hunger calls within the dark.
The orchard waits for hearts to see,
The beauty held in secrecy.

A flicker moves, the shivers start,
In tangled roots, the whispered heart.
With every breath, the orchard sings,
A symphony of hidden things.

Dreaming in the Depths of Earth

In caverns where the shadows loom,
The dreams awaken, freed from gloom.
The soil hums with ancient lore,
A world unseen, forever more.

With every beat, the heart shall trace,
The hidden paths, the secret place.
Down in the dark, where echoes play,
A timeless dance, a bright bouquet.

Each rock and pebble holds a tale,
Of journeys vast that all prevail.
The roots entangle, bind, and weave,
In depth and darkness, hearts believe.

In whispers soft, a promise stays,
To linger through the passing days.
With every breath, the earth will weave,
A dreamwork born for those who believe.

And when the dawn breaks through the stone,
The depths will free what's long been known.
For dreams unearth what time forbids,
And light shall shine where darkness lives.

Beneath the Canopy of Myth

In shadows deep where whispers dwell,
Old tales are spun, like silvered spell.
Beneath the branches, secrets weave,
A tapestry of dreams we cleave.

Moonlight dances on mossy stone,
Where ancient voices feel like home.
The rustling leaves, they hum and sigh,
In the shelter of the night sky.

Creatures of lore in silence creep,
With guardian spirits that never sleep.
They guide the heart through realms unseen,
Where myth and magic reign serene.

Starlit paths through twisted wood,
Echoes of laughter in places good.
A compass forged in the heart's own glow,
Leads the way where few may go.

Embrace the wonder, embrace the dark,
For beneath this canopy, we leave our mark.
In every shadow, a tale unfurls,
Beneath the canopy, the magic swirls.

The Soliloquy of Silent Seeds

In silence, seeds of stories lie,
With dreams and hopes that wish to fly.
Nurtured by whispers of the earth,
They yearn to sprout and prove their worth.

Each droplet hints of tales untold,
In pockets of soil, memories bold.
They sleep and dream in dark embrace,
Awaiting sun's warm, golden grace.

The dance of roots, a hidden art,
Find strength within, yet stay apart.
For every seed, a journey waits,
To break the ground and cross the gates.

With gentlest touch and watchful eyes,
The gardener tends through lows and highs.
In patience lies their solemn creed,
Each silent whisper feeds the seed.

So hear the soliloquy, let it flow,
In forgotten corners, where dreams will grow.
For in the quiet, magic thrives,
In the silent seeds, the hope survives.

Lullabies for the Unplanted

Hush now, dear one, the stars do sing,
For dreams await in the warmth of spring.
Though roots are yet to touch the ground,
In every heart, new life is found.

The petals whisper in soft repose,
While crickets strum their twilight prose.
A lullaby for those yet to bloom,
In moonlit gardens, dispelling gloom.

Embrace the night, with calm embrace,
Feel the rhythm, the cosmic grace.
Although unplanted, you're not alone,
In every murmur, your spirit's grown.

Each twitch of leaf, a distant call,
For morning light to break and sprawl.
When the sun awakens from its sleep,
Dreams will flourish, roots will seep.

So let the lullabies softly weave,
A tapestry of hope, believe.
In slumber's hold, the magic starts,
For even dreams have growing hearts.

Eldritch Tides of the Verdant Crypt

In twilight's glow, where shadows creep,
The verdant crypt holds secrets deep.
Eldritch tides in whispered sighs,
Dance through leaves and sunlit skies.

Forgotten paths where spirits roam,
In every corner, they call home.
Mysteries weave in tangled vine,
Their haunting laughter intertwines.

Roots entwined in earthy lore,
A symphony of life restores.
Each beat a pulse of nature's scheme,
Within the crypt, they gently dream.

The moon, a guardian of the night,
Illuminates the hidden flight.
From depths where silence guards the tomb,
Awakens life in leafy womb.

So delve into the crypt's embrace,
With every breath, allow the chase.
For in each sigh, the magic thrives,
In eldritch tides, true wonder lies.

Lament of the Star-Crossed Seedlings

In the twilight's gentle breath, they sigh,
Roots entwined, beneath the midnight sky.
Their dreams of sunlight, lost in whispered gloom,
A fragile hope beneath the looming doom.

Each petal drops like tears on earth's cold face,
Yearning for the warmth, a tender embrace.
Yet shadows linger where their visions fade,
In silence held, their sweetness, unrepayed.

With every dribble of the weeping rain,
They call for solace, in eternal pain.
The stars above, they twinkle, seeming near,
But distance binds them, wrapped in veils of fear.

Amongst the brambles, hopes are veiled in thorns,
A melody of growth, too often scorns.
Each soft spring breeze carries their lament,
For all the dreams that fate has never bent.

So, let us sow a kindness in their tomb,
And drink in joy where darkest shadows loom.
For even in their grief, they softly sway,
A testament to life's bright, fleeting play.

The Forgotten Vale's Serenade

In shadows deep where whispers weave and wail,
A haunting tune drifts softly through the vale.
The leaves, they dance, in time with twilight's song,
Echoes of a past to which they belong.

Beneath the ferns, where secrets gently dwell,
A glimmer stirs, a tale the winds retell.
The brook's sweet laughter ripples past the stones,
Entwined with ancient dreams and whispered moans.

A phantom's touch can warm the coldest night,
With every sigh, creating purest light.
The vale, it breathes, a heart concealed in time,
Its serenade, a wonder's silent rhyme.

In fading sun, the glow of memories grow,
For lost embraces, 'neath the moon's soft glow.
Each star a promise, brightly set above,
As night unfolds the story wrapped in love.

Thus linger we, amidst the verdant trees,
To drink the magic carried on the breeze.
In forgotten vale, where dreams softly fade,
The serenade of past is ever played.

Chasing Shadows in the Garden

In twilight's grasp, the shadows softly glide,
A dance of whispers where the secrets hide.
Amongst the blooms, their stories intertwine,
As dreams of wonder in the starlight shine.

The roses blush as laughter fills the air,
While ivy trails in play, a gentle snare.
Every corner hides a tale, beguiled,
As crickets serenade the moonlight wild.

With every flutter of a butterfly,
A moment captured, never meant to die.
Their wings like dreams, alight in fading day,
A fleeting glimpse before they slip away.

The candle's glow casts shadows lean and long,
Where echoes linger in a timeless song.
We chase the flitting specters through the night,
In gardens filled with magic's soft delight.

Yet dawn will break, and shadows must retreat,
But memory lingers in the day's heartbeat.
We hold the night within our wistful thought,
A garden's charm, in every moment caught.

Secrets of the Timeless Burrow

Beneath the roots, in earth's embrace, they dwell,
The murmured secrets that the shadows spell.
With every whisper, echoes intertwine,
A dance of moments lost, yet still divine.

The burrow hums with stories long unheard,
Of daring dreams that flutter like a bird.
In soft decay, the wisdom of the old,
Reveals the beauty in the tales retold.

A tapestry of scents, both fresh and sweet,
Where every creature finds a safe retreat.
The paths of ages tread by foot and paw,
Creating maps of life beneath the flaw.

In moonlit nights, the burrow breathes with ease,
As laughter dances on the gentle breeze.
The stars are watchers of the quiet grace,
That roots entwine in nature's soft embrace.

So pause a while, within these ancient walls,
And listen close to nature's tender calls.
For in the burrow's heart, secrets reside,
A timeless wisdom in the earth's true guide.

The Tryst of Untold Flora

In a glade where wild flowers bloom,
Secrets whisper in fragrant plume.
Two lovers meet under moon's soft gaze,
Their hearts entwined in the twilight haze.

Petals dance with the evening breeze,
As laughter mingles with rustling leaves.
Promises made beneath stars so bright,
In a world untouched by common sight.

Faeries flit through the air with glee,
Guiding the brave who dare to see.
Colors unfurl like a painter's dream,
Love's tapestry woven in a silver stream.

Yet shadows lurk where whispers roam,
Caution urged 'midst the fragrant dome.
For in this realm of bloom and light,
Lies a fate that dances just out of sight.

So cherish the hours, sweet and rare,
For time can fade like a perfumed air.
In the quiet grove where hearts align,
The tryst of flora will always shine.

Echoes from the Depths of Twilight

Hushed are the whispers of fading day,
As twilight paints the skies in gray.
Echoes linger from shadows past,
Each secret woven, a spell is cast.

At the edge of night, where dreams take wing,
A symphony of stars begins to sing.
Lost tales echo through the cool night air,
Of love once bold and hearts laid bare.

Faint glimmers dance on the water's face,
Guiding the lost to a hidden place.
In the stillness, the heartbeats sound,
Drawing the weary from hallowed ground.

Yet time flows like a river unseen,
Carving the paths where fate has been.
As dawn approaches with golden light,
The echoes fade, surrendering night.

Hold tightly to whispers, embrace the dusk,
For within the shadows lies hope's sweet husk.
Unearth the secrets of the night's embrace,
Where echoes of twilight leave not a trace.

The Puppeteer of the Serpent's Garden

In a garden where serpents weave,
A puppeteer stirs, with threads he cleaves.
With a flick of wrist, they sway and dance,
Bound by enchantment, caught in trance.

Skins that shimmer in emerald light,
Tempt the wary with a beckoning bite.
Innocence lost, and wisdom gained,
The puppeteer laughs as hearts are chained.

Whispers flutter through the leafy glen,
Secrets shared by the serpent kin.
With each pull of string and silent plea,
The garden blooms with twisted glee.

Yet beware the grip of the unseen hand,
For freedom dwells in a distant land.
Beneath the beauty lies a web spun tight,
In the puppeteer's play, darkness meets light.

So dance with caution, dear hearts so bold,
The serpents may charm, but secrets unfold.
In the garden where shadows easily twine,
The puppeteer's strings may intertwine.

Shadows Lingering in the Perfumed Mist

In a meadow blanketed with gentle haze,
Shadows linger in twilight's daze.
The air, perfumed with secrets told,
Wraps around hearts as the night unfolds.

Beneath the boughs where the dreamers lay,
Whispers arise at the close of day.
Glimmers of hopes in the softest sighs,
As stars awaken in celestial guise.

Through the mist, tales of yore collide,
Fading echoes of love and pride.
Each shadow dances, both wild and free,
In this realm of twilight's mystery.

Yet hidden there, in the curling fog,
Lies the weight of a lingering bog.
For every bloom hides thorns in its fist,
In the shadows that linger in perfumed mist.

So tread with kindness, dear souls who roam,
For the whispers of night may lead you home.
In the garden of dreams where spirits play,
Embrace the shadows, embrace the sway.

Blooming in the Shadows of Giants

In a grove where giants stand,
Soft whispers float like grains of sand.
Petals hide from the sun's bright gleam,
Yet dance in dreams like a secret seam.

Beneath their boughs, the shadows play,
Gentle voices in shades of gray.
Life unfurls with a cautious grace,
Finding beauty in a hidden place.

Roots entwined in a tender race,
Each flower blooms, a soft embrace.
They cast their hopes in twilight's glow,
Unseen wonders thrived below.

With every breeze, the secrets share,
In silent notes of fragrant air.
For even giants must bow and sway,
To the magic of the smaller way.

The Dance of the Starlit Roots

Underneath the silver light,
Where shadows twist in softest night,
Roots awaken from their deep sleep,
To weave a dance that secrets keep.

Entwined in soil, they find their song,
A whispered rhythm, sweet and strong.
Each note they play, a tale of old,
In starlit whispers, bright and bold.

From earth's warm heart, they stretch and sway,
In sync with branches that twist and play.
Together they hum of ancient lore,
A living bond forevermore.

Stars above, a watchful gaze,
Illuminate their tangled maze.
With every pulse, the night ignites,
In unseen dance, their joy unites.

Secrets of the Enchanted Furrow

In furrows deep where dreams are sown,
If you listen close, you'll hear a tone.
Of laughter lost and whispers found,
In the soil's embrace, where life is bound.

Magic flutters on soft winds' breath,
A tapestry of life and death.
Old tales echo, kissed by rain,
Each teardrop hides its joy and pain.

Through tangled weeds, a lesson gleams,
In the quiet hush of midnight themes.
A dance of secrets, rich and rare,
The furrow cradles dreams with care.

Awake, dear heart, and heed the call,
For secrets whisper through the sprawl.
Life's magic flows in every turn,
In the enchanted furrow, we discern.

Requiem for the Hidden Harvest

In twilight's breath, a tale is spun,
Of hidden fields and battles won.
A requiem for dreams once sown,
In silence deep, where hope has grown.

Every grain holds a story's weight,
Of whispered joys and woven fate.
The harvest waits with patient pride,
For seasons' dance, where shadows hide.

Yet through the dusk, we trace the light,
In solace found on quiet nights.
Each root that pushes through the dark,
Holds a flicker, a tender spark.

So gather close, the weary souls,
For hidden harvests claim their roles.
And in the whispers of the past,
We find the strength that's meant to last.

The Serpent's Lament in Silent Herbs

In shadows deep where silence grows,
A serpent weeps, its sorrow flows.
Among the herbs, both wild and tame,
It calls out softly, whispers its name.

Each leaf is touched by its despair,
In moonlit glow, it weaves the air.
With tangled roots and secrets spun,
The herbs hold tales of battles won.

Yet in this realm of vibrant green,
A fragrance sweet, a fatal sheen.
The serpent coils, its heart a cage,
Where wisdom dwells and fear's the wage.

The winds of time blow soft and cold,
As whispers dance, the truth unfolds.
For in the silence, stories weave,
Of love, of loss, of dreams that grieve.

In silent herbs, the serpent's cry,
Resonates with the starry sky.
A lament cast in nature's voice,
Echoes linger, the heart's soft choice.

Echoes of the Forest's Heartbeat

In the forest's depths, a heart does beat,
With whispers carried on the wind's sweet.
Branches sway, a rhythmic song,
As nature's pulse, where we belong.

Leaves shimmer under dappled light,
Each rustle tells of day and night.
Creatures stir, in shadows they loom,
Echoes linger in the thickened gloom.

Through winding paths where dreams collide,
The forest breathes, a world untied.
With every step, the magic grows,
In hidden glades, the heartbeat flows.

An ancient tale of life unfolds,
Of whispered fables, secrets told.
Beneath the stars, the spirits play,
In harmony, they find their way.

A melody of peace does rise,
As nature's song fills all the skies.
The echoes linger, never depart,
The forest's pulse, it beats the heart.

Myths of the Buried Whispered Fruits

In mists of time, the fruits lie deep,
Whispered tales that shadows keep.
Beneath the earth, in quiet embrace,
Legends thrived in this secret place.

Each seed holds dreams of long-lost years,
Of laughter shared and hidden tears.
The roots entangle, stories blend,
In winding paths where histories trend.

A gust of wind brings echoes near,
Of haunted hearts that dance with fear.
In fragrant blooms, the secrets bloom,
As myths unearth the spirit's room.

The flavors rich, so bittersweet,
Like life itself, a complex treat.
In twilight's glow, the fruits reveal,
The whispered dreams that time can heal.

From darkness, hope begins to sprout,
In every bite, the fears cast out.
We taste the past, the future, too,
In buried fruits, the world anew.

The Dance of Nightshade and Fire

In twilight's grace, where shadows blend,
The nightshade sways, a wicked friend.
With petals dark as secrets kept,
In dance with flames, its promise crept.

The fire flickers, a hungry beast,
Drawn to nightshade, a vibrant feast.
Around the hearth, they spin and sway,
A waltz of danger, night and day.

With whispers soft, the embers glow,
As moonlit dreams begin to flow.
In whispered heat, a bond ignites,
Between the dark and radiant lights.

Yet caution sings of shadows near,
For nightshade harbors silent fear.
With every step, a risk embraced,
In shadows cast, the heart must face.

This dance of fate, both bright and dire,
In every twirl, two souls conspire.
Together waltzing, weak and bold,
The tale unfolds, a story told.

Beneath the Verdant Veil

In a glade where shadows creep,
Whispers of the ancient deep,
Leaves that shimmer, softly sway,
Guard the secrets of the day.

Gentle winds with gentle sighs,
Carry tales of lullabies,
Beneath the boughs, where spirits roam,
Nature's heart, a silent home.

Moonlit paths of silver thread,
Guide the wanderers, unsaid,
Dreamers lost, yet never found,
In the veil of life, profound.

Glimmers of forgotten lore,
Bound by roots, forevermore,
Within each petal, truth resides,
Where the world's great wonder hides.

So come and tread the sacred ground,
Let your heart in stillness drown,
For in silence, magic swells,
Beneath the verdant, hidden spells.

Harvesting Dreams from Starlit Soil

In night's embrace, the seeds we sow,
Glimmers of hope in cosmic glow,
With every wish upon a star,
We nurture dreams from near and far.

Soil of silver, rich and rare,
Whispers carried on the air,
Every thought, a twinkling light,
Growing bright in velvet night.

Dancing shadows, swirling grace,
Each small heartbeat finds its place,
In the fields where stardust quakes,
Harvesting all that dreaming makes.

Branches stretching towards the skies,
Bending low with whispered sighs,
Fruit of courage, hope unfeigned,
From the cosmos, love is gained.

In this garden of the night,
Dreams take root, and soar in flight,
With every dawn, a tale unfolds,
In starlit soil, our dreams of gold.

The Withered Echoes of Forgotten Gardens

In shadows cast by time's own hand,
Echoes linger where we stand,
Withered petals, brittle leaves,
Whisper of what nature weaves.

Once a realm of vibrant hue,
Draped in morning's dewy blue,
Now the colors wane and fade,
In the quiet, dreams are laid.

Wind that stirs the silent air,
Carries secrets, light as prayer,
What was lost to ages past,
Yet in memory, holds steadfast.

Beneath the arch of twisted vines,
Remnants sing of sunlit shrines,
Where laughter bloomed and shadows played,
In forgotten gardens, memory stayed.

But hope can rise from ashes gray,
In humble soil, dreams find their way,
For every echo, life prevails,
In the withered, the heart exhales.

Tales of the Blooming Abyss

In the depths where shadows dance,
Lies a tale of fate and chance,
Petals emerge from darkness deep,
In the blooming abyss, secrets keep.

Whispers of the void, alive,
In the quiet, forces strive,
Beauty springs from darkest night,
Starlit dreams ignite the fight.

Twisted roots, a lineage bold,
Stories etched in petals gold,
Every flower tells a tale,
Of loss and love that must prevail.

Through the struggle, life does rise,
Crafting wonders, bold and wise,
In the heart of what seems lost,
Blooms the beauty, no matter the cost.

So venture forth into the night,
Seek the blooms, embrace the light,
For in the abyss, life finds a way,
In the depths, bright blooms hold sway.

Surreal Symphony of Wistful Leaves

Whispers flutter through the air,
As sunlight dances on the grass,
A melody of dreams laid bare,
In twilight's gentle, warm embrace.

Each leaf a tale, a secret spun,
With every rustle, stories told,
Of bygone days and races run,
A symphony of green and gold.

The winds weave through the branches tall,
Creating ripples in the breeze,
A soft, enchanting, ethereal call,
That drifts like laughter through the trees.

Specters of colors swirl around,
In patterns only dreams could trace,
A waltz of joy, a playful sound,
In nature's grand, expansive space.

With every sigh, the evening sighs,
The harmony begins to fade,
Yet in our hearts, the song still lies,
A memory in twilight laid.

Lament of the Ensnared Blossoms

Underneath the silver moon,
A garden weeps with ghostly grace,
Its flowers trapped in timeless tune,
Yearning for the sun's embrace.

Petals heavy with the dew,
Each droplet holds a whispered plea,
To break the chains of night in view,
And dance beneath the willow tree.

The tendrils grip with spectral might,
Gathered close in ivy's thrall,
And though they long for morning light,
Their beauty fades with evening's call.

A chorus swells of hushed goodbyes,
As shadows stretch across the ground,
Their fragrance mingles with soft cries,
In twilight's grip, they are spellbound.

Yet hope remains within their hearts,
For dawn will break this heavy night,
And from the dark, a new world starts,
Replacing sorrow with delight.

Guardians of the Enchanted Orchard

Amid the trees of emerald hue,
Where fruit of every color glows,
The whispers of the ancients brew,
As twilight's gentle magic flows.

Roots that curl like gnarled fingers,
Hold secrets deep within the earth,
Where laughter of the past still lingers,
And every breeze recalls their worth.

The blossoms bloom with tales of yore,
Each petal holds a guardian's dream,
In every flutter, ancient lore,
A bridge between the world and gleam.

They watch as shadows dance and play,
In moonlit silver, bright and bold,
Their silent vows, come what may,
To keep the tales of life retold.

So venture forth beneath their boughs,
And feel the magic in the air,
For in this place, the heart knows how,
To find the dreams that linger there.

The Illusion of the Dusty Canopy

Beneath the arch of ancient trees,
A tapestry of shadows weaves,
With every rustle, a gentle tease,
A whisper in the autumn leaves.

The dusty sky, a canvas gray,
Holds secrets caught in tangled threads,
As sunlight struggles, faint and stray,
To pierce the shrouded paths ahead.

Mirages dance on cobblestone,
Reflecting dreams long cast away,
In this realm, no one is alone,
For echoes of the past still play.

The air is thick with tales untold,
As time itself seems held in thrall,
In shadows deep, the heart grows bold,
An invitation to enthrall.

So wander through this filtered light,
Where fantasy and truth collide,
And in the stillness of the night,
The soul finds solace to abide.

The Undercurrents of Time's Embrace

In whispered flows, the moments sing,
Like silver streams in twilight's cling.
Each heartbeat dances, soft and light,
A shadow weaving through the night.

The path we tread is lined with dreams,
Where every step, a secret seems.
Beneath the surface, stories lie,
As echoes whisper, never die.

The echoes pull, like tides of fate,
In timeless realms, we contemplate.
A tapestry of years unfurl,
As time entwines our hidden world.

Each moment's thread, an artful trace,
In life's grand weave, we find our place.
The essence of our being flows,
Through undercurrents only time knows.

With gentle hands, it shapes our clay,
Through joy and sorrow, night and day.
In time's embrace, our spirits soar,
A journey onward, ever more.

The Veins of Terra's Quietude

In silent woods where shadows play,
The earth breathes soft, in hues of gray.
Beneath the soil, the secrets creep,
Where ancient roots in stillness sleep.

The whispers of the wind ignite,
A lullaby that feels so right.
With every leaf that flutters down,
A story woven through the crown.

The mountains sleep, in blanket deep,
While rivers murmur, secrets keep.
In quietude, the heart can hear,
The pulse of life, so strong, so near.

Each grain of sand, a tale untold,
In whispers soft, both shy and bold.
The very stones, with wisdom weigh,
As time and earth in dance, display.

With every dawn, new colors rise,
In nature's arms, the spirit flies.
In Terra's veins, where silence breathes,
A magic spun through twilight's eaves.

Lullabies for the Earthen Lost

Hush now, dear child, the night is still,
The stars awake, with dreams to fill.
In shadows deep, the soft winds sigh,
A cradle made of night and sky.

For every soul that drifts alone,
The earth will hum, a gentle tone.
Through valleys low and mountains high,
A song for hearts that long to fly.

The forests hold a secret grace,
In every branch, a warm embrace.
In nature's arms, the lost can find,
A solace sweet, a peace of mind.

With lullabies of rustling leaves,
The whispered promise nature weaves.
The moon will guard, through darkest hours,
While dreams take shape like blooming flowers.

So close your eyes and breathe so deep,
In the earth's arms, let worries sleep.
For every star that lights the coast,
Is a lullaby for the earthen lost.

Beneath the Eyes of the Celestial

Beneath the stars, a soft light glows,
In cosmic dreams where silence flows.
The heavens weave a tapestry,
Of distant worlds and mystery.

The moonlight spills like silver ink,
In night's embrace, the heart can think.
With every blink, the cosmos sighs,
A dance of fate beneath the skies.

And through the veil of time and space,
We seek our place, an endless chase.
With every star, a wish is cast,
In whispers soft, our hopes hold fast.

From ancient nights to future dawns,
The universe, a song that spawns.
In every twinkle, dreams reside,
A guide to lead us through the tide.

So gaze above, let worries cease,
In starlit nights, we find our peace.
For under celestial eyes we dwell,
In the heart of dreams, all is well.

Enchantment in the Roots of Time

In ancient woods where whispers twine,
The roots hold secrets, aged and fine.
Beneath the boughs where shadows play,
Time weaves its magic, day by day.

Starlit echoes softly glow,
As twilight blankets all below.
A dance of dreams in murmured grace,
In nature's heart, we find our place.

The breeze, it carries tales untold,
Of heroes brave and hearts of gold.
With every rustle, every sigh,
The magic stirs, and spirits fly.

Roots entwined like bonds of fate,
In silent strength, they resonate.
Among the leaves, the past unfolds,
As mysteries of life are told.

So pause and ponder, take your time,
In the woods where the bells chime.
For every heartbeat, every rhyme,
Is starlit magic in roots of time.

Beneath the Thorns, the Magic Grows

In gardens where the thorns do hide,
A tale of wonder, deep inside.
Amidst the prickles, blossoms bloom,
A secret world, dispelling gloom.

With tender care, the heart must tread,
Through tangled paths, where worries shed.
Each thorn a lesson, sharp yet wise,
Beneath their watch, true beauty lies.

In twilight's glow, the magic sings,
Of delicate hopes on fragile wings.
The night unveils a shimmering dream,
Where shadows dance and starlight gleams.

Even in darkness, light can flow,
For every hardship helps us grow.
Embrace the thorns, let worries fade,
In bravery, true paths are made.

So wander deep where brambles weave,
And find the magic, if you believe.
For in the heart where courage shines,
Beneath the thorns, true love entwines.

Life's Lullaby in the Trampled Earth

In fields long lost to wandering feet,
Life hums a tune, soft and sweet.
Beneath the weight of countless souls,
The earth remembers, life unfolds.

Gentle whispers rise with the dew,
A lullaby old, yet ever new.
With every blade, each grain of sand,
The song of life, both vast and grand.

Though storms may rage, and shadows fall,
Resilience stirs through it all.
In the trampled earth, hope remains,
A pulse of joy, through joys and pains.

Listen closely to the sigh,
Of trembling leaves, the boundless sky.
In every heartbeat, every breath,
Find love and magic, conquering death.

So wander forth with open eyes,
Embrace the dance 'neath endless skies.
For life's a lullaby so dear,
In each soft echo, find your cheer.

Shadows that Kiss the Buried Seed

In quiet corners, shadows creep,
Where secrets lie and stillness sleeps.
A buried seed awaits its chance,
For sunlight's kiss and nature's dance.

The gentle hum of earth's embrace,
Nurtures dreams in a sacred space.
Each whispered prayer, a spark of fate,
In silent patience, we await.

With every drop of dew that falls,
The promise stirs within these walls.
For shadows wrap the seed in care,
A hushed goodbye to doubt and despair.

As winter fades and springtime calls,
The world awakens, life enthralls.
In tender soil, bright hope is sown,
And from the dark, new life is grown.

So trust the shadows in your heart,
They guide the way, they play a part.
For beneath the weight of time and need,
Are shadows that kiss the buried seed.

The Hymn of the Barren Earth

In fields where golden once did sway,
Now silence holds the weary sway.
The echoes of the past will call,
As shadows over hills do fall.

Forgotten are the larks that sang,
And joy in every heart once sprang.
The withered roots in soil lie still,
Awaiting rain to break the chill.

Each gust of wind bears whispered sighs,
Of tales untold beneath dark skies.
Yet hope may dance on weary breath,
And rise again out of this death.

Through barren lands, the heart will roam,
To find a path that leads it home.
For every stone and every thorn,
Holds beauty in its silent scorn.

So sing, O heart, though fields be bare,
In every crack is life's true flare.
For even in the darkest night,
A seed still dreams of morning light.

The Boughs of Forgotten Joy

In woods where laughter once did ring,
The shadows feather soft and cling.
The branches reach with silent grace,
To hide the smile upon their face.

Beneath the boughs of ancient trees,
The rustling leaves tell gentle pleas.
Yet memories, like fleeting rays,
Dissolve within the misty haze.

A fragrant breeze does whisper low,
Of fallen dreams and tales of woe.
In every crack of bark there lies,
A shimmer of forgotten skies.

Beneath the roots, where secrets sleep,
The echoes sway, the shadows creep.
For joy once bloomed in vibrant hues,
Now blushes pale in muted views.

Yet hope may twine with unseen threads,
Amidst the tears, where laughter treads.
For in the heart's most secret nook,
A new song waits, a splendid book.

Beneath the Gnarled Canopy

Beneath the gnarled, old branches wide,
A symphony of whispers bide.
The twilight hums a soft refrain,
Of life spun sweet, of joy and pain.

The earth, adorned with shadows deep,
Holds all the secrets that we keep.
In every rustling leaf, a dream,
Awakens softly, yet unseen.

With tangled roots that grasp the ground,
The silent pulse of life is found.
Each crevice holds a tale untold,
Of weary hearts and spirits bold.

Through tangled thorns, and hidden light,
Resilience blooms in darkest night.
A flicker of what once was whole,
Whispers the strength that lives in soul.

So linger here, 'neath ancient boughs,
Embrace the warmth of life's great vows.
For in this sacred, verdant space,
We find the love that time won't erase.

The Shroud of Perpetual Twilight

In twilight's grip, the world falls slow,
A shroud of dreams begins to grow.
The colors blur, merge into one,
As day gives way, embraces night's fun.

The stars alight on whispered breeze,
In silence wrap their secrets, tease.
For night has tales of shadows deep,
Where ancient memories softly seep.

A sighing mist, a lover's breath,
Caressing all, entwining death.
Yet in the stillness lies a spark,
Of life, a flicker in the dark.

Beneath the veil, the heart will bloom,
Defying echoes of the gloom.
For in the hush, new dreams will rise,
And break the bonds of darkened skies.

So linger sweet, in twilight's sway,
Where whispers fade but night holds sway.
For every end births something bright,
In shrouded realms of secret light.

Beneath the Gloaming Canopy

In twilight's grace, where shadows dwell,
The whispers weave a magic spell.
With leaves that dance in softest light,
We wander forth into the night.

The stars peek through the leafy veil,
While secrets linger, soft and pale.
The moon, a guardian so bright,
Illuminates the world's delight.

Each footstep cracks the twigs below,
The forest breathes, a gentle flow.
A breeze unfolds the tales unspun,
Of love and losses, dreams begun.

Beneath the sighs of ancient trees,
The heart finds solace, wild and free.
In nature's arms, we lose our care,
To find ourselves in whispered air.

So linger here, beneath the night,
Where every shadow cloaks insight.
For in this gloaming, secrets hum,
And magic stirs, as dreams succumb.

Secrets Cradled by the Overgrown

The brambles twist in tangled binds,
With stories lost and truth that binds.
Among the weeds, a treasure lies,
In muffled echoes, silent cries.

The thorns protect what must remain,
A garden filled with joy and pain.
Each petal speaks of time and grace,
In hidden corners, dreams embrace.

A rusted gate, a pathway worn,
Through tangled roots, a tale is born.
The ivy climbs with gentle stealth,
Disclosing nature's hidden wealth.

The air is thick with fragrant spice,
A hint of magic, sweet as mice.
For those who seek with open hearts,
The truth of life with blooms imparts.

In whispered winds, the secrets swell,
Cradled softly, they weave their spell.
To wander through this vibrant gloom,
Is to embrace the wild's perfume.

Rain on the Eldritch Petals

As raindrops fall on petals frail,
A symphony begins to wail.
In every drop, the earth will sing,
Of magic found in summer's fling.

The colors burst like woven dreams,
In nature's dance, the sunlight beams.
Each blossom drinks the night's sweet tears,
Transforming sorrow into cheers.

The storm retreats, but whispers stay,
In fragrant law, the heart will sway.
The ground adorned in emerald hues,
Embraces gifts the rain renews.

Beneath the skies, the world awakes,
In puddles deep, reflection makes.
The petals glisten, fresh and bold,
A tapestry of tales retold.

So let it rain, let tempests call,
For in their wake, the blooms enthrall.
Each droplet writes a book untold,
Of love and life, and hearts of gold.

The Solace of Undisturbed Earth

In quiet spaces, whispers breathe,
The earth holds treasures none perceive.
With roots that delve in gentle sleep,
The world knows secrets it must keep.

The soil, a canvas, rich and deep,
Where dreams lie buried, still, they leap.
A sanctuary wrapped in time,
Where nature hums a silent rhyme.

In dusk's embrace, the shadows lay,
While quiet thoughts begin to sway.
In solitude, we find our worth,
Within the solace of the earth.

Each blade of grass, each pebble round,
Holds echoes of the lives unbound.
To tread upon this sacred ground,
Is to be lost, yet found, profound.

So pause a while, and breathe it in,
The world around is where we begin.
For in the stillness, wisdom's heard,
In the solace of undisturbed.

Whispers of the Languishing Flora

In a garden where shadows play,
Petals sigh in the fading day.
Gentle breezes brush the leaves,
Whispers linger as each one grieves.

Mossy stones hold ancient dreams,
Dewy nights steal silver beams.
The moonlit waltz of ghostly blooms,
Calls forth joy amid the glooms.

Branches bow to secrets shared,
Muted words and glances bared.
Roots entwined in silent trance,
Embrace the dance of night's romance.

Echoes swing in twilight's glow,
Where the heart of nature flows.
Timid blooms in shades of woe,
Hear the songs of long ago.

Yet within the quiet breath,
Lies the beauty born of death.
A cycle spun from life anew,
In whispers held by skies so blue.

The Serpent's Embrace of the Underground

In the depths where shadows crawl,
Serpents weave a silent thrall.
Earth turns soft beneath their glide,
Mysteries held where secrets hide.

Roots entwine in deep embrace,
Veins of life in hidden space.
A whisper travels through the dark,
As serpents leave their silent mark.

Echoed sighs in tunnels vast,
Tell of futures forged from past.
Glimmers glance on scales so bright,
In the weaving of the night.

Silver shadows, coils that twist,
In their paths, the light is missed.
Yet from silence, growth will spring,
Wisdom found in what they bring.

In the layering of the earth,
Lives a story of rebirth.
With each turn, a dance unfolds,
In the dark, the tale is told.

Secrets of the Verdant Watcher

Among the trees, a guardian stands,
Holding life within its hands.
Gnarled limbs stretch to cradle skies,
While wisdom sparkles in its eyes.

Moss-clad roots touch ancient stone,
Whispered truths in echoes grown.
Branches sway, as if to say,
Secrets of the night and day.

With every rustle, tales unfold,
Of life and loss and dreams retold.
In the silence, tales conspire,
Fires born from nature's lyre.

Watchful gaze upon the glade,
Guarding hope that won't soon fade.
Through the seasons, stories flow,
From leaf to ground, from root to glow.

In the stillness, learn to see,
Lessons whispered, soft and free.
The verdant watcher guides the way,
In shadows deep, where spirits play.

Resonance of the Enchanted Soil

Beneath the earth, a song is sung,
In whispers soft, the tales are spun.
Roots tap dance on hidden floors,
Opening wide the ancient doors.

Fruits of labor, nurtured deep,
Secrets shared in dreams and sleep.
Energy flows in currents bright,
Cradled safely by the night.

Rains will fall and storms will break,
Yet the soil holds, for nature's sake.
In every grain, a story swells,
In echoing earth, the magic dwells.

Echoes of life in colors bloom,
Nature's canvas, eternal loom.
From every seed, a world begins,
In enchanted soil, the cycle spins.

So let the heart of earth be known,
In every joy, in every groan.
Resonance lingers, soft and true,
In the whispers of the dew.

Tales from the Rooted Abyss

In shadows deep, where whispers weave,
The roots entwine, their tales believe.
Ancient spirits, hushed and wise,
Guard the secrets, where silence lies.

From caverns cold, the echoes rise,
Of wanderers lost, beneath dark skies.
Their echoes murmur through the night,
In the abyss, out of sight.

With every twist, a branch unbends,
The stories trace where the river bends.
Time does not fade, nor truly flee,
In the realm of the rooted tree.

The earth remembers, every sigh,
Of those who ventured, who dared to try.
Through tangled vines, their fates intertwine,
In shadows deep, their lights still shine.

So listen close, in twilight's hush,
To tales that flicker, in the brush.
For in the depths, where the roots embrace,
Lives a history, a sacred place.

The Lament of the Silent Fertility

In fields once lush, the silence blooms,
Beneath the weight of heavy glooms.
The seeds lie buried, dreams undone,
While whispers fade; no light, no sun.

The fertile ground, a barren shell,
Where prayers go deep, but none can tell.
The hope of harvest lost in pain,
As sorrow clings like autumn rain.

Yet in the dark, a stir of life,
A gentle sigh amidst the strife.
For even still, the roots embrace,
The longing for a warm, bright space.

With each soft breath, a promise made,
That from the dark, new blooms will fade.
Though silent now, the seeds will learn,
To break the soil and softly turn.

So heed the call, in stillness deep,
Where dreams may rest, but never sleep.
For from the heart, new worlds begin,
In every loss, the chance to spin.

Beneath the Dragon's Gaze

Upon the cliffs, where shadows play,
A dragon stirs, in twilight's sway.
With emerald eyes like molten gold,
He watches realms, both fierce and bold.

His breath ignites the evening mist,
A fiery dance, a serpentine twist.
In hushed reverence, the world does pause,
Beneath the gaze, of ancient laws.

Legends weave through moonlit glades,
Of battles fought, of fearless blades.
Yet in his heart, a softer flame,
Yearns for peace, not just for fame.

Through tangled woods, his shadow looms,
In whispered tales, the night resumes.
For every flight, a story grows,
Within the heart, where magic flows.

So heed the night, beneath the stars,
For dragon's gaze reveals the scars.
In every tale, both fierce and bright,
Lies the bond of day and night.

Fruits of the Unseen Realm

In twilight's grasp, the shadows dance,
Where secrets bloom and old souls prance.
The fruits of dreams, in silence grown,
Await the harvest, all alone.

With tendrils soft, they reach for light,
In hidden glades, beyond the sight.
Each fragile bud a whispered prayer,
For those who seek, the brave, the rare.

The unseen realm, where magic flows,
In every seed, a story grows.
From soil enriched by ancient verse,
The promise of a universe.

So gather round, in mystic embrace,
To taste the sweetness, to trace the grace.
For life is but a fleeting stream,
Flowing softly through each dream.

In twilight's hold, the fruits await,
For those with hearts who dare to taste.
In every bite, a world unfurls,
Of unseen magic, of hidden pearls.

www.ingramcontent.com/pod-product-compliance
Ingram Content Group UK Ltd.
Pitfield, Milton Keynes, MK11 3LW, UK
UKHW021516280125
4335UKWH00036B/877